Love Always Remembers

Love
Always
Remembers

A BOOK OF POEMS

by

Joan Walsh Anglund

Random House
New York

Library of Congress Cataloging-in-Publication Data
Anglund, Joan Walsh.
Love always remembers : a book of poems / by Joan Walsh Anglund.
— 1st ed.
p.   cm.
ISBN 0-679-40903-3
1. Love—Poetry.   I. Title.
PS3551.N47L67   1997
811'.54—dc21   97-15971

Random House website address: http://www.randomhouse.com/

Printed in the United States of America
on acid-free paper
2 4 6 8 9 7 5 3
First Edition

For our dear friend,
Connie Boucher

. . . *we will always remember*

Love Always Remembers

In the primer
of Life,
the
first lesson
is Love.

Love
is
the miracle
of
two
becoming
One.

As the tide
   toward the shore,

the movement
   of the Soul
     toward
       Love

 is constant
    and unending.

Wisdom
    dwells in the past,

Hope
    lives in the future,

        but

Love
    abideth in the Now.

Loving hearts
nest easily
. . . together!

Not by riches,
      not by fame,
            not by power,
                  nor beauty,

but
   by your <u>love</u>
          be thou remembered!

The tree of life
　　　has many boughs,

where
　　　the bird of love
　　　　　may perch
　　　　　　　and sing!

Love
  unites
    all differences.

Though we look
          not alike,
  the
    same Love
            is
              within us all!

Life is our schoolroom,

. . . and Love
is always the
best teacher.

Love is Spirit.
    Spirit is Love.

It is eternal
    . . . it cannot age
        nor decay
      nor wither
        nor fade away.

Be aware
    that <u>you</u> are Spirit,

and
    you need have no fear
        of loss
          nor time

    . . . No,
      nor even
        of Death
          itself!

As a window
   to the sun,

keep your heart
   ever open to Love,

  and
    it will come.

Time
    eventually
        breaks
            every wall,
        levels
            every temple,
        erases
            every endeavor

. . . except
        one
            alone

. . . the edifice
        of Love!

See
    . . . with Love,

Act
    . . . with Love,

Give
    . . . with Love,

<u>Live</u>
    . . . with Love!

Two, in love,
        make a new World
                all their own.

The secret is immense,
    we stand in awe
        before its mystery,

yet, too,
    the secret is simple.

One key
    unlocks its power.

Love is the key
    that each man owns,
        but seldom uses.

There is no lack,
   there is only abundance.

All lack begins
   in the mind of fear.

All abundance arises
   from the heart of Love.

Love opens us
        to God's grace,

as the sun
        unfolds the rose
                to her rightful beauty.

It is not
        what we own

    but
        what we love

    that gives Life
              its sweetness.

Love joins all things.
That which separates
is not love, but fear
. . . its opposite.

Love does not exclude,
but opens her doors
wide

. . . to welcome
<u>all</u>!

How shall we find Love?

It is ours
        in that instant

    when
        we give it
            away.

I have taken Love
            with me

    into
        the darkest rooms
                    of sorrow,

    and
        her candle
                has lit my way
                        to Peace.

No joy comes

        to us

    . . . except

        through

            Love.

Speak Love
    and you shall hear love

Seek Love
    and you shall find it

Give Love
    and it shall be returned to you
                a thousandfold.

Where
      is your heart's love?

You must find it,
      for that
         is the <u>exact</u> source
      . . . of all
         your energy,
      . . . of all
         your strength,
      . . . of all
         your force,
      . . . of all
         your <u>life</u>!

Be not deceived,
    though Love is gentle,
            yet it is fierce,
    though Love is soft,
            yet it is strong,

For its force reaches
            past time,
            past death,
            even unto eternity.

And that which
            is done in Love,
                does not die
                but continues forever.

One day
      we must each
            say good-bye
                  to life,

   . . . but
        never
           to Love!

Though Time
           may hurry,

and Death
           may steal,

. . . Love
     always
           remembers.